SHIPPEA HILL

Collected Poems

Dominic O'Sullivan

Shield Crest

ISBN   978-1-910176-31-3

MMXIV

Published by
ShieldCrest
Aylesbury, Buckinghamshire, HP22 5RR
England

www.shieldcrest.co.uk

Also by Dominic O'Sullivan

Icarus in Reverse and other Stories
Undercover and other Stories

Plays:
The Gambler/The View From the Rooftops
Not a Wave Visible and other Plays
Forbidden Fruit and other Plays

Dominic O'Sullivan.

To Peter

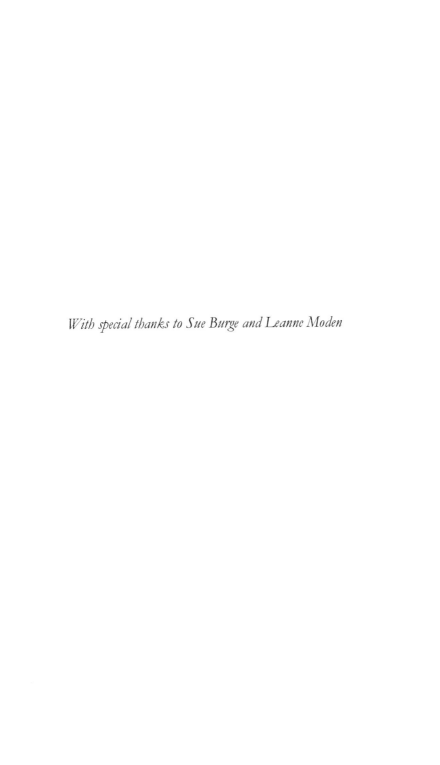

With special thanks to Sue Burge and Leanne Moden

About the Author

Dominic O'Sullivan is a writer of poems, plays and short stories, some of which have been performed at the ADC Theatre, Cambridge, and The Chocolate Factory, North London.

A number of poems in this collection have been performed at the Babylon Gallery, Ely, as part of the Fenspeak Open Mic series and at the Strawberry Fair, Cambridge. Nine poems in this collection are part of the 'In Grendel's Footsteps' project which will be touring Cambridgeshire and the Fens from October 2014 to March 2015.

Contents

Come Live With Me

Come live with me and be my love
And drive your mother round the twist.
Come live with me
And when in bed
We'll have banana splits.
Come live with me
And we'll grow old
But gracefully
Like autumn gold.
Come live with me.

An Invitation

'I wonder,' said the book-trolley lady,
'If any of you would like
To come to church?'

The eyes of the six-bed ward looked on,
Each ensnared by wires of traction,
Pulleys, ropes.

As stranded puppets,
Still and gazing,
We met her eager eye
With staggered incredulity.

The Blue Pudding

It is a long time
Since the blue pudding
Was first created,
When my hand slipped
Momentarily
On the food colouring.

And yet in my dreams
It returns to haunt me,
Indignant at its own creation.

Sword (The Grendel Poem)

The sword is lost,
That of Grendel or of Arthur.
And so the many-headed hydra
That is the English High Street
Lives on,
Defeating us in its uniformity
Its staid solidity of non-variety.
And willingly, as if under the heady haze
Of opium,
We venture forth,
Applaud their coming
And conveniently forget the sword.

Low Slung

The low-slung spider's web
Catches the morning sun.
Small bubbles burst on its innermost threads.
Within, the captive,
Softly wrapped, cocooned and packeted,
A helpless victim to the service
Of necessity.

The Pond

Last night I dreamed of sausages
In my pond.
As the fish were quietly despairing
It seems even our dreams are polluted.

The Laugh

I heard you laugh again that morning.
An echo of remembrance,
Jollity.

But now as we stare at our breakfast plates
The laughs
Are getting fewer.

Rain

I first made love
When the rain came down.
Unexpectedly it was.
A goodnight kiss,
A sudden shower.

The Public Eye

Stolen in mid-stream.
Swollen eyes
From mourning now.

In retrospect, it all seems different
And in our mirrors
We are far from blameless.

The heady scent of flowers and tears
To wash away our guilt.
We gazed one time too many

And with obtrusive eye
Destroyed that
Which we loved.

Meals

Meals on wheels again, my dear!
A sausage bombing along the High Street,
A poached egg gliding through the council estate,
With slightly dusty tasting chips.

Gone are the days of wine and vinaigrette.
Instead the mobile melancholy
Of egg and chips
At half past ten.

Silent

The kitchen is quite silent now.
Forks, knives,
Spoons softly resting
In their slumbering drawers.

No whirrings either
From various machines
Or chopping implements
Or stutting stoves.

And I listen
To the silence.
Breathe it, smell it.
Enjoy its gentle aftertaste.

Judge

The judge took off his outer robe,
His inner garment,
Suspenders, wig.

In the cool nudity
Of night
He was but wafer-thin.

In the Bookshop

Yesterday
I did something
I hadn't done for ages.

As soon as he'd left the room,
Gone to speak to a nagging phone,
I let out a long protracted 'Phwaugh!'
'Phwaugh!' I said
And left.

The vertical bookshelves
Surrounding me
Looked on disapprovingly
As if I had farted
In church.

Windhover

The windhover
Is the kestrel
With its sudden lurch in flight,
A ship listing on a cloudy sea.

And now wind hung
Wind flung
All lies below it,
Carefree, unsuspecting.

After

No callers now.
The Carers neatly stacked away like chairs.
Life extinguished,
Love
Undiminished.

East/West

'I like Germany so much,'
Said the Frenchman
Softly sipping his soup,
'Which is why I am glad
There are two of them!'

Before the Concert

I feed my guests on artichokes,
Each purring contentedly
Into their font-shaped bowls.

Later,
In the cooler moments of washing up,
I picture them
Sitting in their confines of culture
Suppressing farts to string quartets.

Winter

The arena of the cricket field
Is as soft and trim
As a bowling green
Where shapes move even more slowly.

The seats, long emptied,
Show no signs of occupancy.
White flaking paint
Glints in the late autumn sun.

'How was your winter?'
Is the call in spring,
For now is the long, long period of
Hibernation.

Reversal

You realise, sweet Claudine,
As your tenuous hand slips into mine,
That one day it'll be you who guides me
Across this busy, swirling street.

Mozzie

The silent assassin of the night
Whose high-pitched whining
Echoes past my ear.

I reach for the wooden spatula.
My blood spurts out
Across the room.

Goodnight

As I lean up to kiss my younger son goodnight
I notice a vague line
Of stubble across his chin.

As he stoops to return my kiss
I sense a hesitation now,
A moment of self-consciousness.

Gnu

There was a new gnu in the zoo.
Where the old one went to,
No one knew.
The new gnu
Stood on his grassy slope.
Beyond, a hippo sat by a tiny pool.
The world is getting smaller,
Thought the gnu
And caught the hippo's eye.
She did not smile.

Tomorrow

Tomorrow is a grand new day.
My neighbour, Mrs Philips, mishearing,
Came to the meeting
In her birthday suit.

Her pink skin caught the electric light,
Her bottom stuck to the plastic chair.
And yet she stayed unabashed
The whole while through,
Comfortable
In her sartorial elegance.

Canvassing

He comes to my brother's door,
The smiling, effervescent, future
Tory MP.
'We're teachers,' my sister-in-law says.
And in decency, he walks away.

Going Green

Why should the frog
Have all the benefits,
Thought the toad,
And turn into a handsome prince?

And in his bubbling jealousy
He grew another wart.

Pub

Standing in this street-corner pub,
A glass eye stares out towards me.
Behind,
A pike entombed in a slim-line case,
A moose-head crashing through the wall.
It's that kind of place.

Song

Let us sing to pear and apple
Whose fragrant juices make us merry.
Wassail!

Buds bursting forth
In the rite of spring.
Wassail!

Winter forms its cloak of ice,
Its chill breath offering a helpful promise.

E

I am not at home in emails.
There is no 'dear'
And seldom 'love'
And I am a little worried
About punctuation.

Verse

Verse by verse
It's getting worse
And then my mind
Goes blank.

IQ

The poet said it was a Haiku
But I,
Mishearing,
Thought of IQ.
And 'How clever it was,'
I said.

Portrait

Kohl and Honecker
Standing side by side.
Both discredited now
In different ways.

The fat one
Looks as if he could eat the other one up.
Which, in fact, he did
In a way.

Somewhere Else

Cloaked

I visit him now,
The boy around the corner,
Brother John.

I remember the sweet curve of his chest,
The baggy crotch,
The long lean spread of his legs,
All covered now in heavy cloth.
And yet there is the sweet seduction of his eyes.

Bed

I steal like a thief
Into bed.
I do not wish to wake you.
Your soft breath against my cheek.
Love on the horizontal plane.

In Your Element

In real life
You were
As cumbersome
As a seal.
And yet on stage...

F

They should have told him,
The smiling Japanese tenor,
Singing largely to a lunchtime
Concert of office workers,
About the old English *S*,
Which curls itself round
Into an *F*.
'Where the bee sucks, there suck I,'
He should have sung.

Panto

They made the Panto clean
Which some adults thought
Was rather mean.
And the omission of the wobbling Dame
Made it all
Rather
Lame.

Time

There is no time
Like the absent.

Ouse

The River Ouse
Must be quite confoused
For at Earith Bridge,
That's Earith Bridge,
It hives off into three.

They

I am swimming against the incoming tide.
'She should be in a home,' they say.
'Ring an ambulance,' they suggest.
But then swimming,
Floating,
Drifting,
Is better than
Not swimming at all.

Cheek

Love stepped into the darkness,
Kissed me
On the cheek.
I reached out
Into the shadows.

Distraction

You were telling me about your latest home.
I tried to listen
Yet beyond your enthusiastic shoulders
Was the sweetest, sweetest arse.

Tribute

You described yourself as a 'balding salmon'
And yet you wrote
'What will survive of us is love.'

?

Nothing runs it close.
I suppose there's the soft cedilla
And the banana thing
On top of mañana,
(First 'n' of course)
But no,
There's nothing like the subtle slither
Of the serpentine back,
Its explosive aftermath
And silence.

Moon

Tonight the moon is like
A pumpkin
Where silver stars
Lie scattered all around.
I look and gaze
And gaze.

Crutches

I alight from bed after several weeks,
A Phoenix from the ashes,
Or a newborn lamb.
The nurse, gently guiding me,
Causes an erection,
Thereby displacing my centre of gravity.

Waft

A waft of air
And for no reason
I think of you.
The breath of memory
Remembers the very breath.

Iron

They should have told the Lady
Who
Exuberant in her assertiveness
Splayed
Triumphant fingers
The wrong way round.

Unless, of course,
She was being very, very honest.

Bob

I suppose it's strange
If most of your body
Bobs and rises above your head.
But if you're a grey
Or yellow wagtail...

Word

How lovely is the word 'rude!'
How saucy the word 'naughty!'
And yet how ugly
The word 'job!'

Night

Nocturnal emission, it says in Latin.
'Wet dream,' I say, in Anglo-Saxon.
'Ah well,' says the nurse
Answering the rasp of my bedside buzzer,
'This is why we like to have married members
Of staff on duty.'
I watch her bring in the bum-rub trolley
In amazement.

Rustle

There was expectation at the meeting.
They waited patiently for the soft rustle
Of a question
As it reared itself from the floor.
But it never came
And you never asked.

The Manager

'I want to make transparency real,'
The manager said.
'I just can't see it,'
I replied.

In

'At this moment in time...'
He said.
As if there was any other!

Legacy

The first question was in Paradise
On a bright and sunny morning.
'Why don't you eat the apple?'
He said.
She did.

And from that time
Questions have looked like
Serpents
And snakes have lost their
Legs.

I'll Not Know

Kidnap me and let me go
And I'll not know
If I'm in
Reading or in Slough.
Our High Streets are the same right now.

Then

If only the question
Had been raised.
The wandering hands,
The silent altar boys.
But the question never was
As they stifled their qualms in silence.

Bird

I see it bobbing,
Edging over
Tufts of grass,
The wheatear,
Formerly known as 'white arse'
And now anatomically incorrect.

Forty Three

'Never take your gloves off with your teeth,'
Said Miss MacNiece,
Who, on a number forty three,
Saw her teeth fly free.
A lightning flash
And they were in the driver's cab,
Still chattering by his knee.

The Smile

They say that Botox makes you sad
An inability
To smile,
Create a happy face,
Send messages to the brain.

'Ah,' says the other side,
'But if you cannot frown
Dark thoughts are surely banished
And happiness comes
To take its place!

So therefore
With neither smile nor frown
We can't be seen
To be floating up or down.

Oh O!

'That's fine, Mr Sullivan.'
(I won't attempt the other)
'Could I have an apostrophe, please?
And an O?'
A brief silence – wounded, perplexed.
'That's fine, Mr Sullivan.

As It Was

Somehow they cleaned it up
And Prickwill
Gained two extra letters.
Picture it now,
There are no willows,
While wheatear, formerly whitearse,
Flutters by.

The Abdication of Benedict

I'm hardly devout
And less than sporadic
But when the Pope heard
I'd been to Mass,
He said
'I'm off! I've had it!'

First Love

How dark is the fecund soil
Slumbering under an evening sky.
How carefree the word 'fecund!'
Fecund, ripe,
And talking of fecund
Over by the dyke...

Solo Star

With some people
Certain constellations grow,
I know.

But when I am with you
I need no others.
That I know.

Pale

When my brother said
He was going for a shag,
I thought of cormorants,
Their dark shapes hurrying against the sky,
Their water-soaked wings
Dripping under a pale sun.

He would come back home at eleven,
Awash with the smell of cider
And something else.

And as the dark bird
Dipped against the horizon
I realised
I didn't know
My brother very well.

Rail Reversal

I awoke one morning
To find the tracks had gone.
'The Doctor's been,' they said.
'The one whose name's a bit like Leeching.
Gathers arteries, 'they explained,
'Severs, not repairs them.
Came from ICI, a sort of tribe.'

I glanced up the branch line to nowhere,
Felt the wintry breath of isolation.

Onomatopeia

'What's onomatopoeia when it's at home?'
My husband said.
This was after the pub,
Where Guinness makes him grumpy.

He banged the door behind him,
Feet clumping upstairs,
Grunted.
I heard the sound of peeing in the loo
And something worse.

'You are,' I said quietly.

Taken In

It was the
Voice
That alerted me,
Took me in.
I noticed your calmness,
Patience,
Tranquillity.
And then I looked at you,
Slight, handsome, slim.

I felt a tingle,
A frisson,
Gazed
And wanted more.

Progress

They look on with
Incredulity
As if I've been out in the sun too long.
'It's not possible,' they say.
'Not possible.'
'No, no mobile,' I respond.
'I mean, why have something
That stops you in your tracks?'

Second Best

City of dreaming spires,
No, not quite.
It's the other place.

The mighty Isis, the River Cherwell,
No, not quite.
It's the other place.

Rolling hills and stone-clad villages
No, the other place again.

Inspector Morse, Lewis,
Endeavour.
No, no, the other place.
Oldest university in the...
No, the other place.

No wonder, then,
We cannot speak its name,
The place we call
The other place.

Mid Devon/ also Cambridge

'I'm sorry, sir,' the woman said.
'You can't bring that in here.'
(I hate to be called 'sir')
'It's just my apostrophe,' I said.
'I'm sorry, love. They've been abolished.
Done away with.'
(From 'sir' to 'love?')
'By whom?' I asked.
'The Council,' she replied.

A difficult concept, I suppose.
The intrigues of the flying comma,
Defiantly airborne, unfettered, free.
And inwardly I thought,
I cannot join the countrymen
Who long ago
Renounced the O apostrophe.

She stared back blankly.
'In fact, you've just used two
Or three or four,' I said.
She stared back blankly,
Disbelievingly,
A model of intransigence.

Bull

They should have kept quiet about it.
The fact that it once was
A pub.
The white, ceramic plaque
With its impassive macho cow
Only serves to emphasise
The pain of loss.
A whole world on our doorstep
Vanished.

Sleep

The emu sleeps
Some twenty three hours a day
And is a role model
For my youngest son.

Bittern

'We want your land,' they said.
'It's got a bittern,' we replied.
'It's very shy.'
A button? How absurd!
'No, a bittern,' we replied.
'It's very shy.'

'We need the river for our boats.'
'Have you no river where you live?'
We enquired discreetly.
'It's not the point,' they said.
'We come from Cambridge.
We can't be having truck
With simple folk,
Outlying villages, minnows...'

'But we're a city,' we replied.
'And long before you were!'

They looked aghast.
'But we're from Cambridge,'
They replied.

Santa's Pause

'Listen,' they said to Santa,
'We'll do you a deal.
You can live in our department stores
Free of charge!
We'll even pay you!'

Santa thought for a moment.
Everyone has his price.
'It's bloody cold outside,' he said.

Learning Spanish

I was seduced
By the word
'Aseos'
(ah say os)

Was there ever
A lovelier word
For 'toilet'?

Soft

'Soft, my love,' she says.
'You cannot have a courageous cock
Without a wet pussy!'

I close my eyes.
The animals are running riot.

Lady 1

'The Lady's not for turning!'
Was her greatest quote.
Inflexibility hoisted
On its own petard.

Lady 2

'Now,' said the Lady,
Whose advent was still quite new,
'How much is it to buy your souls?'

Souls?

There was a silence,
A pregnant pause.
'If the price is right,' we said.

Lady 3

'I hear,' said the Queen,
'There's another queen around.'
'You mean the butler, ma'am?'
We said.

'No, no, not him!
The one in Number Ten!
She sounds like me.
Get her to change her voice!'

We did,
They did,
She did.

Madam

Madam!
I do not want your dog
Sniffing my anus! Lifting me!

She looks offended
As if I've spat in her soup.
Which, on reflection...

First Sight

I loved you at first sight,
Brought into the world
So tiny.
With unseeing eyes
You clutched my finger,
Grasped it,
Held it tight.

Leicester

Spare a thought for Richard the Third
Buried under a car park
It's really not cricket!
If he'd been at Grace Road
He'd have been under the wicket.

Minus One

Come, take in the magnitude
Of Shippea Hill,
A cool minus one
On most maps.

And as for the elusive hill itself,
Well, look no further,
But look nowhere!

Shippea Hill

Opposite the railway platform
Where one train stopped a day
Was the Railway Tavern
Whose fluttering sign
Squawked like a goose
Over the black fen.

Sadly, the Watney contamination of the time,
Impeded my curiosity
So I never went inside.
A lonely pub at an empty station.
One train a day.
But if I could travel back;
Travel back.

35

Resemble

I see her one evening
On the lower deck of a bus
Red hair
Pale-faced
Head gently wagging,
Elizabeth the First.

As she gazes into the distance
And the bus jolts suddenly,
She is unaware of one of her subjects
Quietly watching.
.

Meeting

All around the room they sat
In shades of deceptive green
The alien rowers,
Sweet sweat of privilege
Dripping from their arms.

They'd come to conquer
Proffering reason, consideration, care,
Said how it would benefit us
To convert our riverbank,
Turn away the inconvenient wildlife.

And once a year, they said,
They'd fly the flag
In some far distant race
And in so doing
Would make us proud.

Curtains

He had the Carers come at four
Or even half past three
To draw the curtains.
Large ladies
To obscure
The healing light of day.
Daily visits now
To offset the chill
And loneliness
Of a world growing darker.

Milk Snatcher

In your wisdom
You withdrew
The free school milk.

A portent of things to come.
A cow with a teat removed.

Harrier

Two birds circled the empty skies,
Darting, floating, majestic,
Unaware of the intrusive eye
Of the restless Prince,
Who, in a moment or two,
Cocked his gun and fired.
There was a sound, then another,
As they tumbled like heavy stones,
Fell into scrubland,
And were scooped away.
Ironic, then,
That these birds of prey
Should share a name
So similar to he who shot them,
Brought about their premature demise,
Concealed behind the dubious banner
Of privilege.

On Missing the Poetry Reading

Sweet nature hath seduced me so
That to the lottie
I did go
And lingering there for many an hour
As doth a bee
To a wholesome flower,

The time it drifted swiftly by
And thus sweet poetry
Neglected I.
A case of tempus *fugit*
(Pronounced like bucket)
Which resembles the expletive
I may have uttered.

Somewhere in Scotland

'Have you peed?'
Said the lady at the door,
Rattling her makeshift tin.
I was unfamiliar with her bowel sounds
(Forgive me, I am Spanish, cannot distinguish
between 'b' and 'v')
Taking up my plate of strawverries
I smiled my berry vest and vurped

Far

I cannot unlove you now.
It is gone too far.
Signed up for the whole deal
On the invisible dotted line.

Ivor (1940)

I write for you
My uncle who
I never knew.

Twenty one he was,
In a TB hospital.
They dropped a bomb.
Our relationship strangled before birth.

When

When you shuffle off this mortal coil
You may well find the angels are on strike.
No celestial lyres to serenade you
Just a murky sort of silence.

For here too, life's accountants
Have had their way
In rationalising, budgeting,
Snipping all away.
And maybe too
On the gates themselves
The portals leading into heaven
A price tag flutters
Gently in the wind.

Gone

Yes, I know he's gone.
Passed on, away,
Whatever you want to call it.

Yet something still makes me
Want to dial his number
Just in case they've got it wrong,
And by the remotest chance...

The Visit

And so it comes to pass
That mum no longer recognises us.
Not me, nor Philip, nor even dad.

As we step out
Into the screeching light of day
I turn and say
'There's somebody in there
Wearing mum's clothes.'

I feel my brother's grip upon my arm
Slowly tighten,
And we would all cry perhaps
But for the moment
The sunlight has dried our tears.

Cold War

I asked my students
One tepid afternoon
What USA stood for.

'Unbelievably selfish attitude'
Said Sergei,
Whose unquestionably
Self-confident appeal
Made it hard to contradict.

'Reasons for your argument?' I enquired.
He just smiled.

Mr Speaker

And so he tells us
Everything in the dementia garden is rosy.

But what about the briars of anger,
The creeping bindweed of forgetfulness,
The often repeated questions?

No, my dear,
When we prick ourselves
On those self-same briars,
We bleed.

Jubbly On the Tube

I took a Jubbly on the Tube,
A solid pyramid of ice,
Sucked out the juice and flavour, orange,
So that there remained
A smaller pyramid of ice.
Then I placed it on the seat opposite
Where it calmly lay in wait.

Virginity

I'm about to lose my stage virginity
Reading to an audience,
You know the kind of thing.

At first it goes okay.
Not bad, I start to think.

But then the book begins to tremble
My legs begin to dance,
And I notice someone
Noticing me!

It's just virginity
I tell myself,
Leaving me,
Having one last laugh.

Gentlemen

Gentlemen – and occasional ladies!
Under the new gay laws,
Designed to further the magnificence
Of the Motherland
We shall no longer be performing Peter Ilyitch
Tchaikovsky.
'Aah!' I hear you say.
But *we* feel
The Nutcracker may have some inner meaning
Which I'm sure we will unravel!
Then there's Mussorgsky with his mother
complex,
(It's just not good enough, Boris!)
And of course Diaghilev
With his Ballet Russe,
Not just the director but Nijinsky too!

So let us sit for a while in contemplation,
Reflect upon our elders' verdict,
Enjoy the prospect of an empty stage.

If

'If,' said the priest,
He of the frequent ruler on our knuckles,
Children's knuckles,
'You hit a priest,
You are automatically excommunicated.'

I am suspicious of this cheap insurance
And at Sports' Day I seize the moment.
Triangular milk cartons there are a plenty
(It's before Thatcher, you see)

From the top of the stands I look down
And I see the self same priest.
So I glance around and toss the carton in the air,
Wondering if it's the milk
Or cardboard, or maybe both,
That will guarantee my exclusion.

I throw it into the air and wait.

The Aftermath

'Fuck it! I missed.

The Evening

The evening
You arrived
The stardust of love
Came down,
Invisibly into the corner
Of one eye,
So that I stumble round
Cliché ridden,
Half-blind.

High

'The church is rather high,' they said.
I gazed at it from the outside,
Was unaware of any particular altitude.

'No, no! High!'
They meant the vicar.
'Is he on the ganja?'
I enquired.

We looked at one another
Two parallel worlds
Of incomprehension.

Barrier

At Bromley-by-Bow's ticket barrier
The West Indian lady on duty
Doesn't believe in our parting handshake.

'Go on!' she says.
'Why don't you give him a kiss?
You know you want to.'

I think for a moment.
It would be rude not to.

Family Plot

My uncle always said
'The Tories would sell your Granny
If they had half a chance!'

And now three cemeteries
Are up for sale.
Westminster Council
Five pee each.
It's beyond the pale!

And oddly
My uncle's words
Are coming home to roost.

Afterwards

I look at the empty bed,
Smooth the creases
Where you have lain,
Where, latterly,
After a surfeit of beer
We lay together,
I half you
And you half me,
Dipping our toes into the unspoken nectar...

Offer

I suggest to the Reverend Father,
He of the Lutheran persuasion,
That I pee into his radiator
To assist the stubborn
Now stationary car.

And yet
Perhaps remembering
That sugar and weed-killer
Can create a homemade bomb,
And fearing other chemical reactions
He politely and discreetly
Declines.

Family Silver

When they said
They'd privatise the line
They told us everything was
And would be fine.

But now the lines are owned
By railways of the State
Of other lands
And I fear it really *is*
Too late
To rectify this great mistake.

Mobile

'How about a mobile confessional?' I said.
'One that follows you around.'

'No,' they said,
Heeding not the need.
'There are psychotherapists and counsellors
For that.'

'But are they free?'
 I asked.

Cricket

'The good thing with cricket,'
Said Jim one evening
As we were waiting at the bus stop,
'Is you don't have to plan your day.'

It was true.
Cricket's three great Acts
Can last from eleven until seven.
The benevolent dictatorship of grass.

Bonjour

Bonjour mes enfants!
The Reverend Mother
From the Mother House
Is paying her annual visit.

She's dressed like a penguin
Armed with a tin of sweets.
She lobs them.

'Bon joo er, ma sher sir!'
We cry.
And thus the spark of language
Is ignited.

Nouvelle

Ladies and gentlemen!
A nouvelle invention.
(It could be the national emblem
Of the Canada)

C'est le poop scoop!
There. Sounds French already!
Utilisez-le!

Snow

I see my mother's Carer
Walking diminutive in the snow.
No buses run across the city
Because tonight it snows.

Muswell Hill to Finsbury Park
Is a long and heavy walk.
Uphill, downhill,
On she treks.

The wind blows colder now.
Nothing to speed the walk.
No buses offer shelter,
Answer,
In the softly falling snow.

Buzzard

The buzzard circles
Aimlessly
It seems
Soaring over
A fruitless landscape
Attended by
A funereal mob of crows.

Winter

'Have you wintered well?'
Is the call in middle spring.
Long,endless, cricketless months.
Silence.
A magazine by the table,
A Radio Times,
A season denied.

Royal Snail

Even the Lady said
'I will not
Privatise
The Queen's Head.'

But now Her Majesty's up for grabs
And by the trough of opportunity
You can see the flocks of grasping hands.

Interruption

Dark is the soil,
Black as night.
'No, no, not quite,' says Bob.
'Night isn't really as dark as it used to be.
Do you know you can see Belgium
From outer space?'

I reflect momentarily on the good fortune of
Outer space.
He's like that is Bob.

Spare

Spare a thought for Richard the Third.
Trashed in life
And now in death.
'My kingdom for a hearse,'
He might have said
But didn't.

North

I remember
When I was young
Our telly
Sometimes said
'From the North – Granada.'

It sounded like another country.
I went there
And it was.

Shame

'It's a shame,' said the Councillor
Confidentially.
'You know, about the cathedral.'

I thought of its fallen arches,
Henry's followers,
Cromwell stabling his horses...

'It would make an ideal site for a supermarket,'
He added.
'Up on the hill,
Restored to its rightful place.
For at present our Superstores
Do sadly languish in the shadows.'

I gazed in admiration.
This was the man
Who gave us W.H. Smug
And Smartbucks,
Alas now sadly departed.

'But never fear,' he continued.
'We shall build shopping malls
To be the *new* cathedrals,
Whose gates, whose portals
Will be open, available for all!
And out of respect, of course,
We shall name them
Cloisters, Spires and Heavenly Moments.'

And in that second
I loved the Council
And all it stood for,
For they understood the very nature
Of our souls.

Love Song

You are beautiful,
You are wise,
I love your smile,
The colour of your eyes.
That surely should suffice.

Farewell

So, farewell then, Mr Biggs,
Co-star with the Sex Pistols!
You did it your way
Or so you say.
But if you'd grabbed a railway franchise
You could've robbed us blind
On each and every day!

Time's Winged Artichoke

Frustrations of the world subside
When I'm at my cabbage's side.
The gentle orbs of palest green
Into my hands
Do slip and preen.

Yet at my back
I always hear
Time's thunderous traffic
Scurrying near.

The black soil
Will soon be washed away.
The cabbage
That so prospered
Will have had its day.

I

Technology
Sounds like an illness,
The I-Pad
A swelling
We have to scratch.
Till one day,
Festering,
It will burst forward
And swallow us.

Russia's Greatest Contribution

'Yes, it's true,' said Lars.
'We Vikings are of Russian stock.
And one day
We *did* sail far away
To the place they call America.'

'But after careful consideration
And much deliberation,
And the odd folk-tune,
We decided not to say anything,
For discretion is...
Simply drifted away,
Kept stumm, as some might say.
But then the Europeans came...'

Trains

To miss you twice
Is a bereavement.
Travelling backwards
Instead of forwards.
Defeated by the vigours
Of work,
Circumstance, time.
And the unspoken words
Have drifted into vapour.

Mr K

'Talk to the IRA,' he said.
There was an outcry
But they did.

'Cheap fares for everyone.'
Overruled, of course,
By a bunch of unelected fools.

And now they replace him
With a fluffy clown
Whose golden hair catches the sun.

This poem is done.

Humour

I love the humour
Of a fart,
Which in its many guises
Bursts forth,
A convivial messenger
Of vulgarity.

Haydn

Haydn sat down to tea.
He was all congeniality.
There was a knock at the door.
Duh-duh-duh-duh!
'That'll be Beethoven,' he said.

Ely Post Office

The post office
Has ended up
In a car park.
But personally
I would have put it
In a lavatory
Where the odours of privatisation
Run sweet.

Cromwell

It's Tuesday evening,
Ely in the seventies,
And the only restaurant open
Is The Cromwell.

I think the Lord Protector,
Puritan-clad, warts and all,
Would be dismayed, outraged,
To find he's the only source of entertainment.

Deep

They said the man in the chip shop
Was given over to metaphysical
Contemplation.
'Is he a deep fryer?' I asked.

Sprinkle, Sprinkle

Sprinkle, sprinkle,
The white death is coming,
Pure as the driven snow;
Softly over dubious chips,
The over-chilled salad
Never destined to have a taste.

Its powerful ally
Lies within the Burger Bun
With its cocktailed fats
And its MRM

Sprinkle more,
Keep going...
You're nearly done.

Socks

The smell of socks
Lingers in the room
As fragrant as an old fart.
Congealed breadcrumbs in the sink
Spread fast like lichen on a tree.

When he lived
And loved
She opened windows,
Cleaned and tidied,
Let in the morning air.
But now everything,
The room with windows shut
Lies buried
Like a tomb.

Trees

Trees in the winter sun
Dark, naked along the riverbank,
Let branches scrape against the clouds.

Beneath them all
Lies torpor,
A world that's half-asleep,
While two-legged animals,
Unaware of the reviving sun,
Are fretting over presents, cards,
The company they're forced to keep.

Cormorant

I wondered if the cormorant,
Wings spread beside the riverbank,
Was parodying the eagle,
You know, on those flags and stamps,
The documents of State.

His wings spread further,
Reptile turning into bird,
Dark feathers drying
In violent gusts of wind.

Flour

I put a worm into a saucerful of flour
And waited
For it to fart.
'There,' I said to my mum one morning.
'If they can do it,
Why not you?'
But she was steadfast
If not resolute
In her denial.

Creek

Brandon Creek sounds a trifle bleak,
Makes me think of Ambrose Bierce and
misanthropy.
Feltwell sounded better
Till I saw the polished husks
Of hostile planes.
So I settled for Six Mile Bottom
And in a simultaneous vision
Saw Mrs Biggs,
The illustrious 'bedder'
Of Porterhouse Blue.

'What's in a name?' I hear you ask.

Enclave

'Won't be long,' they said.
'Just for a while.'

Maybe sixty years isn't too long
For barbed wire compounds,
Settlements,
Which hide 'unspoken' things.

And now the contents
Are where they shouldn't be
And weapons drift beside the sea,
Defiling marsh and coast alike.

Dare we say
'It's time to go'
In our best politest tone?
We'd even try
'It's been nice knowing ya.'

Wink

I love the collusion of a wink
Whose temporary bond
Is as fleeting
As a flock of darting goldfinches.

Pity

It's a shame
Your boyfriend cannot converse.
All I see is a blank wall
An empty screen.
I wait for the lights to come on,
Quietly hoping.

Stuck in a Lift with Mandela

'Do you remember me?'
The most famous man in the world said.

Stuck in a lift
A few welcome moments of captivity.

He smiled.
A flimsy box awash with greatness.

From Outside

From the street
You can see the lights come on,
Flashbuds of inspiration,
Nocturnal poems.
But one day there'll be a power cut.

RAF Hospital Ely

It's the folly of our age
To knock down hospitals
Put houses in their place.

Yet those who dwell inside
Will be so fighting fit
They'll never need a doctor,
Let alone a first-aid kit!

Never

'Never underestimate
The stupidity of the electorate'
My enlightened friend once said.
He never really worked.
Didn't believe in it
Was deeply suspicious,
Last worked as a bouncer
Weeley Pop Festival
1972

Recently he celebrated
A jubilee of no work.
Then expired.
Whereupon, I suppose,
He really is retired.

Calcite Rhombohedra

Sounds like a rampant garden shrub
But the reality
At repose
Under a smoothly polished case
Is an exercise in immobility.

Map

I look at the map
Rejoice at the fact
That we are most entirely
An island

'We were once joined to France'
My granddad said,
'But that was many years ago.'

Blissful was the rejoicing,
Great indeed perhaps,
When the waters came
To grant our happy severance.

To Lis

From mountain to black fen
My thoughts are with you now
As they were then.

Journey to Wisbech (Haiku)

Reeds shivering
Long dykes keep reappearing
Car fall over maybe

Some Think

Some think the old are another species
Locked up in period clothes
With names like Edna, May or Cecil.

Yet it was only yesterday, it seems,
They laughed and climbed
Jumped on each other's backs,
Fornicated in the shrubbery.

What Is?

'What is this?' I asked.
'Jus,' they said.
(Jus with Northern vowels)

The waiter
With his knobbly fingers
Worn away, no doubt,
By many dishes,

Pointed to the menu.
Ah, jus!
Surely some letters missing?

Yet when it came
It was all but gone,
A brief trickle
Hinting at its existence,
And like the letters, too,
That were,
It also had evaporated.

Journey to Shippea Hill

Southery is but northerly of Ely
So east I went
To Prickwillow
Which, in politeness,
Gained its last two letters
From sanitising Victorians,
Till I reached the vertiginous heights of
Shippea Hill.
So, on the platform I asked
Where the hill might be?

'Yer standin' on it, yer daft bugger!'
Came the reply.

Walking

'Come to London
Get covered in fucking mud!'
My friend from Kent complained.
Took taxis everywhere
No wonder he looked pained.

And now
From an eternal Medway cloud
Looks down at us on high,
Sees us covered in fucking mud
And laughs.

The Fens are Flat (Six Poems)

1

They say the Fens are flat
But you always cycle uphill
Wind against you.
Illusional, delusional, confusional.

2

The Fens are flat because they took away
What might have been.
Yet on my hill of Ely
I feel a sense of elevation, of well-being.

3

Fen.
So many drugs end in *fen*
Triptofen, Neurofen, Ibuprofen,
Offering the promise of false escape.

4

The Flens are fat because I'm tripping over words

5

The Fens are flat because they always were
But then they made them flatter still
Taking away the water
With its scope for movement,
Offering the promise of reedy escape.
The Romans did it first
(Normans hadn't a clue.
Bribed the monks of Ely.
Everyone has his price)
Then the Dutch,
Vermuyden came,
Vermeiden – to avoid,
No means of escape
Flattening everything like dough,
Turned a fertile land
Into a bread-basket.

6

The Fens are flat because nothingness isn't there'

Shark

Sweet is the steel-like structure of the shark
Whose body and components
Mean it's forever on the move.
See it glide and dart.
And as if by jealousy motivated
We fire a gun, a dart, harpoon, whatever
And bring aquatic grace
To ungainly rest.

Ode to a Bed-pan

The new slipper bed-pan
Promises greatly.
See it effortlessly slide
Under the bed-bound rump,
Listen to the sound
Of its gentle music,
A feast of fond arpeggios.

And, as it says under the rim,
'If a flannel cap is made for the blade
Fastened by strings
Under the handle,
Considerable comfort
Will be afforded.'
Ah, bliss!

Left Alone (Assembled from pictures)

Tractor, abandoned; the land laughs.
I see shapes dance around its forgotten hulk,
Like the house behind it, windowless eyes.
Both of which stand unburied,
As a shape, portly, a man with a beer-belly,
Waits on a branch line to nowhere,
Dreaming of long lost voices.

Boathouse Blues

'Would the otter please follow the signs
And vacate to the other side?'
The otter,
Seeing it was Cambridge,
Seat of learning,
Participant of occasional
Boat Race
Duly obliged.
Now who says nature isn't on our side?

Notes

Page 1: 'Come Live With Me'.   Acknowledgements
to Christopher Marlowe.

Page 1: 'An Invitation'. I am grateful to the Norfolk
and Norwich Hospital when it was at St
Stephen's for their excellent care.

Page 4: 'The Public Eye'. Written after the death of
Diana, Princess of Wales.

Page 5: 'Meals'. Meals on Wheels may now be
defunct.

Page 7: 'After'. In memory of Pamela O'Sullivan.

Page 11: 'Canvassing'. As happened on my brother's
doorstep in Palmers Green. I think the MP
involved now hosts television railway
journey programmes.

Page 12: 'Song'. With many thanks to the generosity
of the Pickled Pig Cidermakers, Stretham,
near Ely.

Page 13: 'Somewhere Else'. This poem is somewhere
else.

Page 15: 'F'. As recounted by the Reverend Ronald T.
Englund of St Ann's Lutheran Church,
Moorgate.

Page 19: 'Iron'. The Lady in question may also have
quoted St Francis of Assisi.

Page 24: 'As It Was'. Prickwillow, formerly Prickwill,
near Ely.

Page 24: 'The Abdication of Benedict'. The very next
day!

.

Page 51: 'Snow'. In memory of Daphne Thomas, an exceptional lady.

Page 56: 'Time's Winged Artichoke'. With acknowledgements to Andrew Marvell.

Page 58: 'Mr K'. To Ken Livingstone.

Page 60: 'Cromwell'. The former Cromwell Restaurant, Fore Hill, Ely.

Page 60: 'Sprinkle, Sprinkle'. MRM stands for Mechanically Recovered Meat.

Page 64: 'Enclave'. At the time of writing U.S. air bases are still operational at Mildenhall and Lakenheath.

Page 65: 'Stuck in a Lift with Mandela'. I am indebted to John Humphrys for his anecdote on the BBC Today Programme.

Page 66: 'RAF Hospital, Ely'. The only hospital that didn't smell like a hospital. The level of care was invariably excellent.

Page 66: 'Never/Walking'. In memory of Dave Smith, a learned man.

Page 67: 'Calcite Rhombohedra' is an object in the museum.

Page 68: 'Journey to Wisbech'. One of nine poems which were written in Wisbech Museum as part of the 'In Grendel's Footsteps' project.

Page 68: 'What Is?' Sometimes the language of menus is worrying.

Page 72: 'Shark' and 'Ode to a Bed-pan' are all objects in the museum.

Page 73: 'Boathouse Blues'. We only hope the otter will oblige.